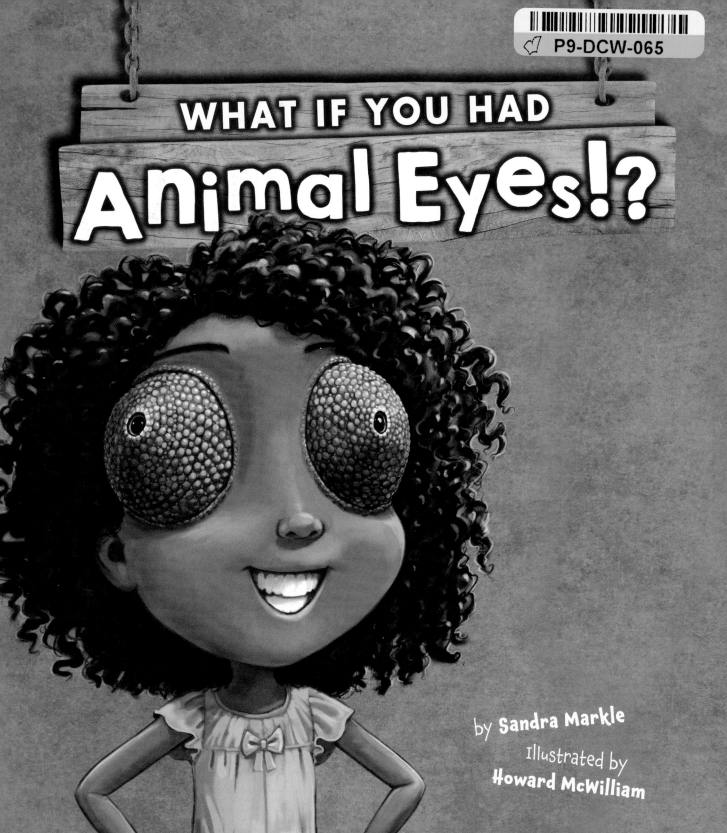

WHAT IF YOU HAD
Animal Eyes!?

by Sandra Markle

Illustrated by
Howard McWilliam

Scholastic Inc.

For Nancy
VandenBerge
and the children
of Dr. E.T. Boon
Elementary School,
Allen, Texas

Photos ©: cover top and throughout: Dim Dimich/Shutterstock; cover bottom right: Kuttelvaserova Stuchelova/Shutterstock; cover background: martinhosmart/iStockphoto; back cover: HaywireMedia/Shutterstock; 4: Hiroya Minakuchi/Minden Pictures/Getty Images; 4 inset: Oliver Britton/Shutterstock; 6: Dopeyden/iStockphoto; 6 inset: Alex Hyde/Minden Pictures; 8: Pobytov/iStockphoto; 8 inset: kurt_G/Shutterstock; 10: kwiktor/iStockphoto; 10 inset: JOEL SARTORE, NATIONAL GEOGRAPHIC PHOTO ARK/National Geographic Creative; 12: Karl R. Martin/Shutterstock; 12 inset: Treat Davidson/Minden Pictures; 14: Worldfoto/Dreamstime; 14 inset: William Jr/Getty Images; 16: Picture by Tambako the Jaguar/Getty Images; 16 inset: Richard Du Toit/Minden Pictures/Getty Images; 18: Kat Bolstad/Seapics.com; 18 inset: Norbert Wu/Minden Pictures/Getty Images; 20: Owen Franken/Getty Images; 20 inset: Pablo Hidalgo/Dreamstime; 22: Mark Kostich/iStockphoto; 22 inset: Ivkuzmin/Dreamstime; 24: Veronika Peskova/Dreamstime; 24 inset: Vitaly Titov/Dreamstime.

Text copyright © 2017 by Sandra Markle
Illustrations copyright © 2017 by Howard McWilliam

All rights reserved. Published by Scholastic Inc., *Publishers since 1920.* SCHOLASTIC and associated logos are trademarks and/or registered trademarks of Scholastic Inc.

The publisher does not have any control over and does not assume any responsibility for author or third-party websites or their content.

ISBN 978-1-338-10108-9

17   21

Printed in the U.S.A.   40
First edition, September 2017

Book design by Kay Petronio

What if one day when you woke up, the eyes on your face weren't yours? What if, overnight, a wild animal's eyes took their place?

CHAMELEON

A chameleon's eyes stick out like twin telescopes. These cone-shaped bumps are actually fused-together eyelids that are open just enough to peek through. This limits the chameleon's view, but these eyes can do something tricky. Each eye moves separately. That way, the chameleon can look for prey, such as crickets, in two directions at once!

FACT

When a chameleon spots prey, it focuses both eyes on it. That way, it doesn't miss catching a meal.

If you had chameleon eyes, you could look around the toy store fast to find exactly what you want.

GOLDEN EAGLE

A golden eagle has laser-sharp vision. This bird can see up to eight times better than most people. It can also spot its prey up to two miles away. In a flash, the golden eagle can shift its eyes from focusing on something far away to something up close. This is perfect for keeping an eagle-eye on—and catching— a fast-hopping rabbit.

FACT

A golden eagle's eyes have a third eyelid that sweeps across the eyes like windshield wipers, keeping them clean.

If you had
golden eagle eyes,
you could sit up high
in the stadium and still
see the football game.

DRAGONFLY

A dragonfly's eyes are huge! They have to be, because each dragonfly eye has up to 30,000 tiny lenses. A human eye only has one. Scientists aren't sure how a dragonfly's brain creates images from all of those lenses. But they do believe having so many lenses lets the dragonfly spot movement fast. That's how a dragonfly can see a flying mosquito in time to catch it!

FACT

A dragonfly has three small, extra eyes that help guide its flight path by sensing bright light and shadows.

If you had dragonfly eyes, you would be a star reporter because you'd never miss any of the action.

CLOUDED
LEOPARD

A clouded leopard's eyes have a special mirror-like layer at the back. This layer reflects light back through the retina, the part of the eye packed with light-sensing cells. This helps the clouded leopard see well in the dim light at nighttime. That mirror-like layer is also what makes the clouded leopard's eyes seem to glow.

FACT

The clouded leopard has slit-shaped pupils (openings where light enters the eye). These can expand about 100 times to let more light in. A human's round pupils only expand about ten times.

If you had clouded leopard eyes, you'd never be surprised in a dark haunted house.

BULLFROG

A bullfrog's eyes are on top of its head, so the frog can hide underwater and still watch out for enemies. Its eyes are also wide apart. That way, a bullfrog can see nearly all the way around itself without turning its head. But these eyes help a bullfrog do more than just see! When a bullfrog swallows, it closes its big eyes. Its eyes sink down through openings in its skull and help push meals down its throat.

FACT

A bullfrog's eyes each have a third, see-through eyelid. When a bullfrog dives underwater, these eyelids slide over its eyes—the perfect built-in swim goggles.

If you had bullfrog eyes, a blink would let you swallow a **BIG** bite.

FOUR-EYED FISH

A four-eyed fish really has only two eyes, but each eye has two different parts. Each of these four eye parts has its own *pupil*. This fish keeps half of each eye underwater, looking for the insects and smaller fish it eats. It keeps the other half of each eye above the water, watching for birds and other predators that are after a fish dinner.

FACT

Four-eyed fish usually travel in groups called schools. So there are always lots of eyes watching in every direction.

If you had four-eyed fish eyes, you could read while riding your bike and never take your eyes off the road.

YELLOW MONGOOSE

A yellow mongoose's eyes have rectangular pupils. These give it a very wide view of its world. That means the mongoose can easily spot insects and lizards to catch and eat. It also keeps watch for hunters, such as jackals, sneaking up from the far left or right. When there is danger, its special eyes also help it spot escape routes. The yellow mongoose is mainly active during the daytime when it can see best.

FACT

To see farther and peek over bushes, the yellow mongoose stands up tall on its hind feet.

If you had yellow mongoose eyes, you'd always win at laser tag.

COLOSSAL SQUID

A colossal squid has the biggest eyes in the world. Each eye is as big as a soccer ball! At the back of each eye is a part that produces its own light. It's like having built-in flashlights that are always on and glowing brightly. This makes it easy for the colossal squid to find fish to eat, even though it lives deep down in the ocean where it's always dark.

FACT

Scientists can't take photos of living colossal squid because they live so deep underwater. Our closest peek is seeing their cousin, the giant squid. But their eyes can't produce light!

giant squid

If you had colossal squid eyes, you could go on nighttime hikes without a flashlight.

LLAMA

A llama has black, bubble-like crystals that form a fringe at the top and bottom of its pupils where light enters the eyes. In bright sunlight, these crystals turn into bands that stretch across the pupils. These bands block so much light from entering the llama's eyes that it's like having built-in super-dark sunglasses. A llama's thick, bushy eyelashes also make great sunshades.

FACT

A llama's extra-long eyelashes let it feel when it is getting close to something so it doesn't get poked in the eye.

If you had llama eyes, you wouldn't be blinded by the bright spotlights during your big solo.

DESERT HORNED VIPER

A desert horned viper's eyes have clear eyelids that do not open or close. That means this snake can't blink to clean its eyes—but it doesn't need to. Its eyelids work like safety goggles. Because it lives in hot deserts, the viper usually waits until it's cooler at night to go hunting. Then this snake's slit-shaped pupils open wide so it can find a mouse or lizard for dinner.

FACT

Each time a desert horned viper sheds its scaly skin for a new one, it gets new, clear eyelids, too.

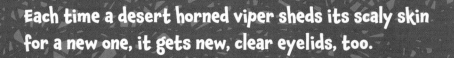

If you had horned viper eyes, you wouldn't need safety goggles to do science experiments!

TARSIER

A tarsier's eyes are a huge part of its little body. Its giant eyes and large pupils are perfect for hunting tiny insects during dark nights. A tarsier can't move its eyes because of how its skull bones support them. Luckily, it can turn its head far enough around to look over its shoulder and see what's behind it. That way it can keep an eye out for predators, such as wild cats and large snakes.

FACT

Each of a tarsier's giant eyes weighs more than its brain.

If you had tarsier eyes, you could easily watch for base stealers in time to throw them out!

Wild animal eyes could be fun for a while. But you don't need your eyes to light the way or to look in two directions at once. And you never use your eyes to spot something two miles away or to help you swallow your dinner.

So if you could keep wild animal eyes for more than a day, which kind would be right for you?

Luckily, you don't have to choose. Your eyes will always be people eyes.

They'll be what you need to read books, check out the stars at night, and see the people you love all of the time.

WHAT'S SPECIAL ABOUT YOUR EYES?

Your eyes work with your brain to help you see. Light enters your eyes through your pupils, the black spots in the center of the colored part of the eye (the iris). Your eyes work best when the amount of light entering your eyes is just right. In bright light, your pupils get smaller to block light out. In dim light, your pupils get wider to let in as much light as possible. Once light enters your eyes, it passes through the shiny, clear lens of the eye.

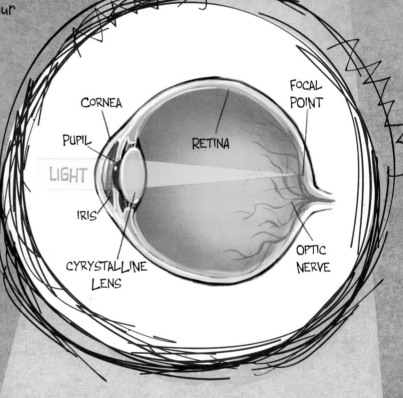

CORNEA

PUPIL

LIGHT

IRIS

CYRYSTALLINE LENS

RETINA

FOCAL POINT

OPTIC NERVE

From the lens, light travels through a clear jelly that fills the inside of the eye. It goes all the way to the layer at the back called the retina. The retina is made up of special, light-sensitive cells. When light reaches these cells, it triggers them to send signals to your brain. Your brain figures out those messages quicker than a blink, and it sends out its own signals to let you understand what you're seeing.

KEEP YOUR EYES HEALTHY

Here are some tips for taking care of your eyes.

• Be careful to keep anything—even your fingers—from touching your eyes.

• Wear glasses if you need them to help you see better.

• Wear protective eyewear during sports activities and science experiments.

• Wear sunglasses whenever you're outside—even when it's cloudy.

• Have regular checkups with your family's eye doctor.

WHAT IF YOU HAD
Animal Teeth!?
by Sandra Markle
Illustrated by Howard McWilliam
SCHOLASTIC

WHAT IF YOU HAD
Animal Hair!?
Sandra M...
Illustrated by
Howard McWilliam
SCHOLASTIC

WHAT IF YOU HAD
ANIMAL FEET!?
Sandra Markle
Illustrated by Howard McWilliam
SCHOLASTIC

WHAT IF YOU HAD
Animal Ears!?
by Sandra Markle
Illustrated by Howard McWilliam
SCHOLASTIC

WHAT IF YOU HAD AN
Animal Nose!?
by Sandra Markle
Illustrated by Howard McWilliam
SCHOLASTIC